BRITISH
WARSHIPS
& AUXILIARIES

The ageing Type 42 destroyers and their Sea Dart missile systems remains the RN's frontline Air Defence asset.

THE ROYAL NAVY

Time for a change....

Having edited this book each year since 1979 the time has now arrived to pro-
mote Steve Bush to become the full time editor - and of our bi-monthly magazine *Warship World* too (twenty five years in any job is enough for anyone!).
He has been doing much of the work for a few years now and I am more than
happy to let him take this job on and put his own personal fingerprint on its con-
tents. I am not retiring (two daughters at University!!) or anything like it for the
moment!

It is good to hand over when our readership is increasing and no one is more
surprised than I at the orders we get for this book from around the world as we
seek to give an independant overview of the Royal Navy and it's all important
auxiliaries each year....

I'm sure Steve, with his long naval career behind him and proven editing expe-
rience, will only improve the book many of you have come to appreciate since
that very first issue. Thank you for your loyalty - long may it continue!

Mike Critchley
Publisher

Approaching this, my first introduction, I was of a mind to look back at the very
first edition of *British Warships & Auxiliaries*, published in 1979 and see how the
Royal Navy has fared over the intervening years.

In 1979 the Royal Navy was operating 173 front line warships (supported by
29 RFAs). In the intervening years 122 new vessels have been accepted into
service (12 new RFAs) and 210 have been paid off (22 RFAs). As we enter 2004
Royal Navy frontline strength stands at 84 ships (supported by 19 RFAs).

It is true that the world has changed. The Cold War, which required the operation of large scale blue water anti-submarine assets, has been consigned to
the history books and, following the terrible events of 9-11, focus has shifted to
the war on terror and to larger scale rapid reaction expeditionary operations in
littoral waters.

THE PAST (THE FIRST BW&A INTRODUCTION - as published in 1979)

*In the year that sees HMS ARK ROYAL paying off and heading for the scrap-
yard the Royal Navy is without its own fixed wing aircraft at sea for air support
of a task force. The Navy now has to rely on shore based aircraft of the Royal
Air Force for 'overhead' fighter cover— until HMS INVINCIBLE and her aircraft*

are operational at sea in a couple of years time.

As the large fixed wing carriers leave the Navy, and with her amphibious force severely cut, the capital ships of the fleet become the highly sophisticated nuclear powered 'hunter killer' submarines. These submarines now form a large part of the fleet whilst their half sisters - the conventionally powered boats - diminish in numbers. An announcement is awaited regarding their replacements.

This year sees the arrival of the 'all missile frigate' - the Broadsword Class - to boost the Royal Navy's anti-submarine forces that are the envy of many NATO navies. Even so, more anti-submarine vessels would be required to keep the deep-sea sea lanes of the Atlantic open in time of tension or all out war. This year the Lynx helicopter will be replacing the ageing Wasp in many of these frigates which will give them a much better 'punch' for anti-submarine and anti-fast patrol boat operations.

Cause for concern however exists in the Royal Navy's Mine Countermeasures forces. As an island nation, unlike our European neighbours, we depend heavily on our merchant marine to bring industry's raw materials and the nation's food to these shores. It is a sobering thought that Britain, as the world's greatest importer of food, requires a merchant navy to bring 98% of that food for the national larder. A few well placed mines could well disrupt this flow of materials and food into our major ports. With 55 million mouths to feed, such a situation could rapidly become a major national problem in this country.

From over 120 minesweepers in the 1950s, less than 40 remain today - and their highly expensive replacements are slow to arrive and will not be available in great numbers. As more ships retire of old age the Navy could well be in an embarrassing position in a few years time by having only a handful of ships available. One can only hope that our NATO allies will be able to provide the ships to keep our ports open in any emergency as it is questionable whether the Navy will be able to cope with a serious mining threat.

The 'small ship fleet' of the Navy is now greatly depleted - with only one operational Patrol Boat (TENACITY) and the Bird Class of Patrol craft having proved an expensive mistake. We thus rely entirely on NATO for ships of this type should they be required. Hovercraft have been given exhaustive trials and a Hydrofoil will be evaluated next year—but no firm order for the former has been placed, despite nearly 10 years of trials.

It is easy to be critical of the capability of the Fleet - but in a country that spends far more on its Social Service budget than on national defence, the Navy of today is as effective as possible under the financial restraints imposed. A few years ago long term expenditure was cut drastically and even with a change of government now, many items axed then would take years to replace - should any future government decide to do so. With a warship taking anything from 6 to 10 years from initial conception to being operational at sea one can only hope we, as a country, are not 'found wanting' should outside pressures be brought to bear on our nation.

The following pages give a brief insight into the variety of ships which form the fleet-it should be remembered however, that they are never all available at one time, as refits, docking and maintenance periods are essential to keep the modern warship in operational readiness.

THE PRESENT DAY

The previous twelve months have been very much a test of character for the Royal Navy and I am bound to say that it has performed admirably.

At the start of 2003 the Navy faced two huge demands for its resources. A threatened firefighters strike saw much of the fleet alongside in port with its crews deployed around the country to provide fire cover. At the same time the

RN was also quietly preparing for war.

Against a background of anti-war sentiment in much of the World - including the UK - the RN quietly realigned a long planned Far East deployment and began to make war preparations. The deploying ships were augmented by a significant amphibious element and the fleet slipped out of ports around the country on what was still advertised as a routine Far East deployment. Although this played nicely into the hands of the politicians, who did not want to be seen to be turning up the heat either in the Gulf or with the anti-war lobby, it did mean that the naval contribution was largely ignored by the media. True, there was speculation - but little was confirmed until the Task Group - the largest assembled since 1982 and the Falklands War - arrived in the Gulf, by which time war was pretty much a foregone conclusion.

Once in area the RN s contribution was again largely overshadowed by events ashore. The ARK ROYAL (operating as an LPH) and OCEAN were both instrumental in landing the Royal Marines on the Al Faw peninsula in the opening hours of the land battle, both by helicopter, and landing craft based in Kuwait - conducting the first opposed airborne amphibious assault since Suez. It must also be remembered that the Royal Marines are very much a part of the RN - a fact lost on the public.

The nuclear powered submarines SPLENDID and TURBULENT were instrumental in using their Tomahawk land attack missiles to strike at Iraqi targets. TURBULENT was returning home from a Far East deployment when she was diverted to the Gulf. Having fired her missiles she was released to resume her journey home. SPLENDID, however, was reloaded twice in area - another first - and at one time, during disputes about overflying rights, was one of only a small number of Tomahawk equipped submarines available to the coalition. Although the exact number of missiles fired has never been officially admitted by the MoD it is known to be over thirty.

The frigates CHATHAM, RICHMOND and MARLBOROUGH were also instrumental in the success of the land operations on the Al Faw peninsula, providing naval gunfire support in positions close inshore. CHATHAM was also the voice of Radio Free Iraq broadcasting radio messages directly to the Iraqi people - perhaps the first time that psy-ops had been conducted from an RN ship.

That the amphibious vessels and their escorts were able to get so close to Iraq was down to the work of the smaller ships in the Task Force. The large MCM force cleared the northern waterways and the coastal survey vessel ROEBUCK operated close inshore to the Iraqi coast charting deep water to enable the LPHs to move significantly further north during the subsequent landing operations.

Not to be forgotten are the unsung heroes of such an operation - the support services. Over 75% of the RFA fleet was deployed in support of these operations, as well as four of the six Strategic Sealift Ro-Ro vessels and countless ships taken up from trade. Warships were successfully sustained at sea in an operational state for extended periods (119 days at sea for EDINBURGH!) with only three of the ships requiring repairs that couldn t be done at sea.

Once more, the RN has provided a major contribution to a joint military operation - operating a long way from home and out of the public eye. It is sad that the RN participation will probably be remembered more for the loss of 849 NAS aircrew in the wake of the Sea King collision rather than any of the above - an indictment of what the media feels is more newsworthy - but the RN can, and should, be justifiably proud of their achievements during this campaign.

Now, as the ships have returned to the UK and they begin to regroup, how is the RN faring? Without doubt the current fleet is overstretched as it constantly tries to juggle the commitment, manpower and hull availability equation. The large shipbuilding programme is promising much, but in this post Iraq war period there are many rumours that the Treasury is seeking stringent cuts across all of the Armed Forces. As we went to press (Nov 03) the much delayed Defence White Paper was yet to be published. MoD officials are preparing the ground for what many fear will be bad news whether that be cuts in programmes, operating costs or capability is still open to debate - but something it seems is going to have to be sacrificed.

With the RN already feeling the pressure in terms of meeting commitments any cut in operational capability is going to be a bitter pill to swallow - especially in the wake of the Iraq War.

Areas for concern remain. The three CVSs are coming to the end of their operational lives, with INVINCIBLE scheduled to pay off into reserve for the last time in 2006. But until the long awaited CVF arrives in 2012 they will continue to operate without a dedicated fixed wing air-defence fighter.

The nuclear powered submarine fleet is gradually recovering from earlier traumas, with several boats emerging from prolonged refits and others being given a clean bill of health following the faults found in their reactor cooling systems. In 1998 the Strategic Defence Review announced a reduction in SSN numbers to 10, indeed, SPLENDID paid off in 2003. However, problems with the Astute programme may see this dip to only half a dozen submarines if the current decommissioning schedule is adhered to (from which total you must subtract those in refit or maintenance). Hardly a credible force!

An almost constant concern is the number of escorts - decreasing numbers of ships and increasing commitments find the escort force worked harder than ever before in peacetime. The knock on effect is that ships (and crews) become tired and require ever more maintenance - increasing the work load on the remaining ships - and so the cycle goes on. There is no reserve waiting in the wings - in time of war you cannot generate new escorts as has happened in previous wars - they are just too sophisticated. The grounding of NOTTINGHAM caused a drop in escort numbers until she is repaired. Despite the MoDs persistence that she has been replaced by GLASGOW, and therefore there is no loss in operational numbers - it must be remembered that she was not a reserve ship - but one of the 32 escorts to which SDR reduced the fleet (since further reduced to 31 with the sale of SHEFFIELD).

But perhaps of the greatest concern in these days of the world terrorist threat are our dwindling MCMV forces. Reduced to just 22 vessels under SDR, with three of those assigned to patrol duties and another at extended readiness, and unlikely ever to return to service, this force would be totally inadequate to deal with any serious mining threat to our island nation. The resources in men and equipment thrown into the effort to open just one sea lane into Iraq in 2003 show the size of the potential problem. There is no longer an RNR MCM Squadron and again no reserve ships to boost front line forces in time of need.

The area where we can easily and cheaply boost our defences is in Coastal Defence. The ageing Island class vessels have been replaced by newer more capable hulls - but so far only three have been acquired - which for a nation that relies so heavily on the sea for trade is woefully inadequate. Innovative deployment of some of the P2000 patrol craft for security operations around Gibraltar and Cyprus have given these small vessels an operational purpose at last. Despite their poor seakeeping in inclement weather, is it not time to deploy the remaining vessels in a similar role around our own ports?

THE FUTURE

The future should be rosy, with a large replacement programme underway - Nuclear Submarines, Aircraft Carriers, Escorts, Tankers, Amphibious ships. However, it is not for us to predict when these new ships will enter the fleet.

Being recently promoted to editor, I thought that I should treat myself to a new car. I decided that it would be best to adopt the SMART approach to procurement, providing a list of specifications, capability and budget to various suppliers. I had a basic specification in mind. It would need to be four door (wide-opening and comfy seats for my ageing frame), 1800cc engine, economical, blue in colour, delivery in two months and less than £15k. Having given my specs out I received several offers and plumped for ACME Motors Plc, who said they were up to the job. A week after accepting the contract they informed me that for my £15k I could only have a three-wheeled, second hand, two door rust bucket with a very dodgy engine, but I would have to wait for a year! I declined the offer - but, I feel MoD in similar circumstances would perhaps have accepted! Maybe a little extreme but it seems to be the way that SMART procurement operates - Industry and not the customer setting the goalposts.

As a layman in this field, I see two approaches to Defence Procurement. Give your specs out to industry, chose a preferred bidder and buy the product. If the preferred bidder moves any of the goalposts - more money, less capability - go to the next bidder. Your product should be dictated by what you require - not by what industry feels it should supply.

The second is to buy a product off the shelf - something already designed and in production. The MEKO family of corvettes and frigates are so successful because the basic hull and design work is all done and the customer can select from a range of options to fit their requirements. VT Group are another company who successfully design, build and market. Look at how painless the River class acquisition has been.

With budgets bound to be reduced and purse strings tightened can we really afford the luxury of spending millions on endless rounds of assessment phases before metal is ever cut for a new vessel?

Defence Procurement programmes have historically been expensive and protracted affairs but surely it doesn t have to be like that. SDR was published in 1998. A cornerstone of that document was to realign our Armed Forces into a Rapidly Deployable Force capable of supporting littoral operations and amphibious expeditionary warfare, anywhere in the world. And key to that policy was the acquisition of two large aircraft carriers for power projection and air defence of the fleet. As we enter 2004, the MoD and its preferred bidder are still arguing about the design - which is getting smaller by the day - and have already spent millions of pounds. The last big UK carrier project, CVA-01, started in the same manner - and that never got built in the end! A firm grip will have to be taken on all of these capaital programmes, CVF, Astute, Type 45 if we are going to have them enter service in anything like the numbers, or with the capability we need. You can be sure that the Treasury is looking very closely at the expenditure and will jump at any excuse to get programmes curtailed or even cancelled.

Perhaps with the limited budgets that will be available to the RN we should seriously look at alternative options for capital expenditure. For too long the RN has been stuck in the old school of escorts being the jack-of-all-trades. This might have been the case in the Second World War when relatively cheap escorts could turn their hands to Anti-air, Anti-submarine, general patrol and escort work. But in the first part of the 21st Century this is far from the case. Todays RN escorts are highly sophisticated, highly specialised and dreadfully expensive warships. It doesn t make sense to have half of these high-technology vessels patrolling the waters around the Falklands, hunting drug-runners in the Carribean or interdicting oil smugglers in the Gulf.

If the RN is to have a Rapid Deployable Expeditionary Support Group, perhaps it is time to focus on providing the assets for this front line capability on a permanent basis. Acquire sufficient ships so that there will always be an Expeditionary Support Group, comprising your Aircraft Carriers, Amphibious

Units, Submarines, Escorts and Support Ships, and have them operate as a cohesive unit, always fully worked up as a group ready to deploy.

Second line tasks, such as the Falkland Islands Patrol Ship and West Indies drug interdiction role can then be carried out by more utilitarian ships, perhaps with interchangeable, palletised weapons systems so that they can be re-roled for different deployments. The VT group have just unveiled plans for such a ship, a helicopter patrol frigate. There would be no development costs, just the cost of acquiring an off the shelf capability. In this way the RN might be able to meet its worldwide commitments and still have a formidable, rapidly deployable punch whenever and wherever it is needed.

As this is written the future for the RN might indeed be bright. There is much to be optimistic about. There is the prospect of some major new tonnage in the pipeline - just how much of it will see the light of day will depend on the long delayed Defence White Paper and the Treasury. But there are still serious issues to be addressed.

Procurement and programme management needs to be scrutinised and drastically overhauled. There are no longer the budgets available for cash to be squandered with no visible sign of progress.

Operational requirements need to be re-assessed in the light of probable lower operating budgets. Should the RN be seriously looking at operating a two tier navy to get the best out of what will be limited resources?

Will any UK Government ever really give National Defence the priority and budgets needed to protect this island nation or will it forever be a Cinderella to the bigger departments, accepting the leftovers after Health, Education and Social Security have fed from the Treasury trough?

I would like to think, that in 25 years time when looking back at the first half century of *British Warship & Auxiliaries*, that many of the long term concerns had been addressed. It would be nice to see a significant coastal patrol force securing our ports and approaches. It would be nice to see a credible MCM force capable of maintaining clear sea routes to the main UK ports. It would be nice to see escort numbers swollen by a new class of utilitarian patrol frigates and it would be nice to see two new large aircraft carriers complete with an air defence fighter.

But none of this will be possible if we can t attract the right calibre of person to join (and more importantly stay in) the Royal Navy.

As long as the RN operates away from the public gaze, it will be hard to get the youth of today fired up for a career in the Navy. Navy Days are few and far between, high street RN Careers Offices are a thing of the past and together with the loss of the Royal Tournament and Field Gun competitions, the RN has a very low public profile. The decision to allow uniform to be worn ashore again will help raise public awareness of the RN, but what is needed is good PR beamed into peoples living rooms showing what the RN does once it sails over the horizon. Documentaries this year following the ARK ROYAL during Operation Telic and *Civvy to Sailor* charting the progress of new recruits were a step in the right direction, but so many of the interviews were with disgruntled, bored and I d rather be somewhere else ratings.

This year sees the start of a new television drama series *Making Waves* charting the adventures of the crew of the fictitious HMS SUFFOLK. Made with the backing of the RN, if it is anything like the 1970s *Warship* series, it might just start to get the message across. Lets hope that it paints a representative picture of RN life and encourages the youth of today to head for the careers office!

Steve Bush
December 2003

SHIPS OF THE ROYAL NAVY
Pennant Numbers

Ship	Pennant Number	Page	Ship	Pennant Number	Page
Aircraft Carriers					
INVINCIBLE	R05	13	MARLBOROUGH	F233	18
ILLUSTRIOUS	R06	13	IRON DUKE	F234	18
ARK ROYAL	R07	13	MONMOUTH	F235	18
			MONTROSE	F236	18
Destroyers			WESTMINSTER	F237	18
			NORTHUMBERLAND	F238	18
NEWCASTLE	D87	16	RICHMOND	F239	18
GLASGOW	D88	16			
EXETER	D89	16	**Submarines**		
SOUTHAMPTON	D90	16			
NOTTINGHAM	D91	16	VANGUARD	S28	10
LIVERPOOL	D92	16	VICTORIOUS	S29	10
MANCHESTER	D95	17	VIGILANT	S30	10
GLOUCESTER	D96	17	VENGEANCE	S31	10
EDINBURGH	D97	17	TRENCHANT	S91	11
YORK	D98	17	TALENT	S92	11
CARDIFF	D108	16	TRIUMPH	S93	11
			SCEPTRE	S104	12
Frigates			SPARTAN	S105	12
			TRAFALGAR	S107	11
KENT	F78	18	SOVEREIGN	S108	12
PORTLAND	F79	18	SUPERB	S109	12
GRAFTON	F80	18	TURBULENT	S110	11
SUTHERLAND	F81	18	TIRELESS	S117	11
SOMERSET	F82	18	TORBAY	S118	11
ST ALBANS	F83	18			
CUMBERLAND	F85	20	**Assault Ships**		
CAMPBELTOWN	F86	20			
CHATHAM	F87	20	OCEAN	L12	14
CORNWALL	F99	20	ALBION	L14	15
LANCASTER	F229	18	BULWARK	L15	15
NORFOLK	F230	18			
ARGYLL	F231	18			

Ship	Pennant Number	Page	Ship	Pennant Number	Page
Minehunters			PURSUER	P273	26
			TRACKER	P274	26
BRECON	M29	21	RAIDER	P275	26
LEDBURY	M30	21	BLAZER	P279	26
CATTISTOCK	M31	21	DASHER	P280	26
COTTESMORE	M32	21	TYNE	P281	24
BROCKLESBY	M33	21	SEVERN	P282	24
MIDDLETON	M34	21	MERSEY	P283	24
DULVERTON	M35	21	SCIMITAR	P284	25
CHIDDINGFOLD	M37	21	SABRE	P285	25
ATHERSTONE	M38	21	PUNCHER	P291	26
HURWORTH	M39	21	CHARGER	P292	26
QUORN	M41	21	RANGER	P293	26
SANDOWN	M101	22	TRUMPETER	P294	26
INVERNESS	M102	22			
WALNEY	M104	22	**Survey Ships & RN Manned Auxiliaries**		
BRIDPORT	M105	22			
PENZANCE	M106	22	GLEANER	H86	31
PEMBROKE	M107	22	ECHO	H87	29
GRIMSBY	M108	22	ENTERPRISE	H88	29
BANGOR	M109	22	ROEBUCK	H130	30
RAMSEY	M110	22	SCOTT	H131	28
BLYTH	M111	22	ENDURANCE	A171	32
SHOREHAM	M112	22			
Patrol Craft					
EXPRESS	P163	26			
EXPLORER	P164	26			
EXAMPLE	P165	26			
EXPLOIT	P167	26			
LEEDS CASTLE	P258	23			
ARCHER	P264	26			
DUMBARTON CASTLE	P265	23			
BITER	P270	26			
SMITER	P272	26			

• MoD/CROWN COPYRIGHT   **HMS Victorious**

VANGUARD CLASS

Ship	Pennant Number	Completion Date	Builder
VANGUARD	S28	1992	VSEL
VICTORIOUS	S29	1994	VSEL
VIGILANT	S30	1997	VSEL
VENGEANCE	S31	1999	VSEL

Displacement 15,000 tons (dived) **Dimensions** 150m x 13m x 12m **Speed** 25 + dived **Armament** 16 - Trident 2 (D5) missiles, 4 Torpedo Tubes **Complement** 132

Notes
After the first successful UK D5 strategic missile firing in May '94 the first operational patrol was carried out in early '95 and a patrol has been constantly maintained ever since. These submarines have two crews each to maintain the maximum period on patrol. Construction costs of the last, VENGEANCE, are estimated at £863 million. VANGUARD entered refit at Devonport in February 2002 and is due to complete in April 2004.

HMS Triumph

TRAFALGAR CLASS

Ship	Pennant Number	Completion Date	Builder
TRENCHANT	S91	1989	Vickers
TALENT	S92	1990	Vickers
TRIUMPH	S93	1991	Vickers
TRAFALGAR	S107	1983	Vickers
TURBULENT	S110	1984	Vickers
TIRELESS	S117	1985	Vickers
TORBAY	S118	1986	Vickers

Displacement 4,500 tons **Dimensions** 85m x 10m x 8m **Speed** 30 + dived **Armament** 5 Torpedo Tubes **Complement** 110.

Notes

Quieter, faster and with greater endurance than the Swiftsure class. Tomahawk Cruise Missiles fitted in TRIUMPH, TRAFALGAR and TURBULENT and TRENCHANT. It is expected Tomahawk will eventually be fitted in all of these boats by 2007. Decommissioning dates announced by the MoD remain: TRAFALGAR (2007); TURBULENT (2008); TIRELESS (2011); TALENT (2017); TRIUMPH (2019); TORBAY (2021) and TRENCHANT (2023).

• DAVE CULLEN

HMS Sceptre

SWIFTSURE CLASS

Ship	Pennant Number	Completion Date	Builder
SCEPTRE	S104	1978	Vickers
SPARTAN	S105	1979	Vickers
SOVEREIGN	S108	1974	Vickers
SUPERB	S109	1976	Vickers

Displacement 4,500 tons dived **Dimensions** 83m x 10m x 8m **Speed** 30 knots + dived **Armament** 5 Torpedo Tubes **Complement** 116.

Notes
All are based at Faslane. Tomahawk is fitted in the heavily modified SPARTAN, which it is believed also has the capability to deliver Special Forces. SPLENDID was decommissioned on return from operations off Iraq in 2003 and is laid up at Devonport. Decommissioning dates announced by the MoD remain: SOVEREIGN (2005); SUPERB (2006); SPARTAN (2006) and SCEPTRE (2010).

• CHRIS ROGERS

HMS Invincible

INVINCIBLE CLASS

Ship	Pennant Number	Completion Date	Builder
INVINCIBLE	R05	1979	Vickers
ILLUSTRIOUS	R06	1982	Swan Hunter
ARK ROYAL	R07	1985	Swan Hunter

Displacement 20,700 tons **Dimensions** 206m x 32m x 6.5m **Speed** 28 knots **Armament** 2 - 20mm guns, 3 Phalanx/Goalkeeper **Aircraft** 8 - Sea Harrier, 12 - Sea King / Merlin **Complement** 682 + 366 Fleet Air Arm.

Notes
Recent practice has seen only one carrier operational. ARK ROYAL recommissioned in November 2001. INVINCIBLE returned to the fleet in May 2003 following a £65 million refit at Rosyth. ILLUSTRIOUS entered refit at Rosyth in November 2002 and is scheduled to return to service in 2005. It has been announced that INVINCIBLE will be placed at Extended Readiness from 2006. All can assume the LPH role. Vessels frequently deploy with RAF Harrier GR7s.

13

HMS Ocean

LPH

Ship	Pennant Number	Completion Date	Builder
OCEAN	L12	1998	Kvaerner

Displacement 21,578 tonnes **Dimensions** 208m x 34m x 6.6m **Speed** 17 knots **Armament** 3 x Phalanx, 6 x 30mm BMARC guns **Complement** Ship 284, Squadrons 180, Embarked force 800.

Notes
Can carry 12 Sea King and 6 Lynx or Gazelle helicopters. Frequently employed as the flagship of the UK Amphibious Ready Group. RAF Chinook helicopters are normally carried as an integral part of the ship's air group, but they are unable to be stowed below decks. During a docking period at the end of 2002 she was modified with two 50m blisters attached to the hull at the waterline below the after chine to improve safety margins while deploying LCVPs from the after davits.

14

• MIKE WELSFORD

HMS Albion

LPD
ALBION CLASS

Ship	Pennant Number	Completion Date	Builder
ALBION	L14	2003	BAE Systems
BULWARK	L15	2004	BAE Systems

Displacement 18,500 tons, 21,500 tons (flooded) **Dimensions** 176m x 25.6m x 6.1m
Speed 18 knots **Armament** 2 x CIWS, 2 x 20mm guns (single) **Complement** 325
Military Lift 303 troops, with an overload capacity of a further 405.

Notes
The first of two LPD(R)s ALBION arrived at Devonport on 3 April 2003 and commissioned on 19 June. Vehicle deck capacity for up to six Challenger 2 tanks or around 30 armoured all-terrain tracked vehicles. Floodable well dock, with the capacity to take either four utility landing craft (each capable of carrying a Challenger 2 tank) or shelter a US Landing Craft Air Cushion (LCAC). Four smaller landing craft on davits, each capable of carrying 35 troops. Two-spot flight deck able to take medium support helicopters and stow a third. The Flight Deck is capable of taking the Chinook. Does not have a hangar but has equipment needed to support aircraft operations. Has deisel/electric propulsion. Sistership BULWARK is not now expected to be delivered before July 2004.

15

• STEVE BUSH

HMS Exeter

DESTROYERS
SHEFFIELD CLASS
(Type 42) Batch 1 & 2

Ship	Pennant Number	Completion Date	Builder
NEWCASTLE	D87	1978	Swan Hunter
GLASGOW	D88	1978	Swan Hunter
EXETER	D89	1980	Swan Hunter
SOUTHAMPTON	D90	1981	Vosper T.
NOTTINGHAM	D91	1982	Vosper T.
LIVERPOOL	D92	1982	C. Laird
CARDIFF	D108	1979	Vickers

Displacement 3,660 tons **Dimensions** 125m x 15m x 7m **Speed** 29 knots **Armament** 1 - 4.5-inch gun, 4 - 20mm guns, Sea Dart Missile System: 2 - Phalanx, Lynx Helicopter, 6 Torpedo Tubes **Complement** 266.

Notes
GLASGOW returned to service in 2003 to replace the damaged NOTTINGHAM. NOTTINGHAM was returned to UK on 8 December 2002 after sustaining severe hull damage in Australia. She underwent a £26million repair at FSL Portsmouth, scheduled to complete in April 2004. The following decommissioning dates announced by the MoD remain: NEWCASTLE (2007), CARDIFF (2008); GLASGOW & LIVERPOOL (2010); EXETER (2011); SOUTHAMPTON and NOTTINGHAM (2012).

HMS Edinburgh

SHEFFIELD CLASS
(Type 42) Batch 3

Ship	Pennant Number	Completion Date	Builder
MANCHESTER	D95	1983	Vickers
GLOUCESTER	D96	1984	Vosper T.
EDINBURGH	D97	1985	C. Laird
YORK	D98	1984	Swan Hunter

Displacement 4,775 tons **Dimensions** 132m x 15m x 7m **Speed** 30 knots + **Armament** 1- 4.5-inch gun, 2 - Phalanx, 2 - 20mm guns, Sea Dart missile system, Lynx Helicopter, 6 Torpedo Tubes **Complement** 269.

Notes
Stretched versions of earlier ships of this class. Designed to provide area defence of a task force. Deck edge stiffening fitted to counter increased hull stress. GLOUCESTER returned to service in July 2003 following an 18 month refit at Devonport. YORK and EDINBURGH (only) to be fitted with 4.5-inch Mod 1 gun. The MoD confirmed the following decommissioning dates: MANCHESTER & GLOUCESTER (2013), EDINBURGH & YORK (2014).

FRIGATES
DUKE CLASS (Type 23)

Ship	Pennant Number	Completion Date	Builder
KENT	F78	2000	Yarrow
PORTLAND	F79	2000	Yarrow
GRAFTON	F80	1996	Yarrow
SUTHERLAND	F81	1997	Yarrow
SOMERSET	F82	1996	Yarrow
ST ALBANS	F83	2001	Yarrow
LANCASTER	F229	1991	Yarrow
NORFOLK*	F230	1989	Yarrow
ARGYLL	F231	1991	Yarrow
MARLBOROUGH*	F233	1991	Swan Hunter
IRON DUKE*	F234	1992	Yarrow
MONMOUTH*	F235	1993	Yarrow
MONTROSE*	F236	1993	Yarrow
WESTMINSTER	F237	1993	Swan Hunter
NORTHUMBERLAND	F238	1994	Swan Hunter
RICHMOND	F239	1994	Swan Hunter

Displacement 3,500 tons **Dimensions** 133m x 15m x 5m **Speed** 28 knots **Armament** Harpoon & Seawolf missile systems: 1 - 4.5-inch gun, 2 - single 30mm guns, 4 - 2 twin, magazine launched, Torpedo Tubes, Lynx Helicopter (Merlin in LANCASTER) **Complement** 173.

Notes
These are now the backbone of the RN's frigate force. They incorporate 'Stealth' technology to minimise magnetic, radar, acoustic and infra-red signatures. Gas turbine and diesel electric propulsion. Those ships marked * have been fitted with the Mk 8 Mod 1 4.5-inch gun. The rest of class to be fitted by 2011. Type 2087 Sonar is to be fitted in 12 of the class.

HMS St Albans

HMS Monmouth (complete with Mk8 4.5-inch Mod 1 gun)

HMS Cumberland

BROADSWORD CLASS
(Type 22) Batch 3

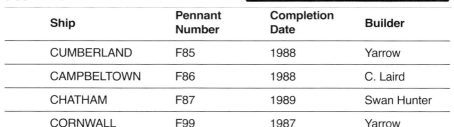

Ship	Pennant Number	Completion Date	Builder
CUMBERLAND	F85	1988	Yarrow
CAMPBELTOWN	F86	1988	C. Laird
CHATHAM	F87	1989	Swan Hunter
CORNWALL	F99	1987	Yarrow

Displacement 4,200 tons **Dimensions** 147m x 15m x 7m **Speed** 30 knots **Armament** 1 - 4.5-inch gun, 1 - Goalkeeper, 8 - Harpoon, 2 - Seawolf, 2 - 20mm guns, 6 Torpedo Tubes, 2 Lynx or 1 Sea King Helicopter **Complement** 259.

Notes

All these ships have an anti-submarine and intelligence gathering capability. All are capable of acting as fleet flagships. CUMBERLAND fitted with Mk8 4.5-inch Mod 1 gun in 2001 and the remainder will be fitted by the end of the decade. SHEFFIELD, the last of the Batch 2 Type 22s, was withdrawn from service in October 2002 and commissioned into the Chilean Navy in September 2003 as ALMIRANTE WILLIAMS. BRAVE and BOXER are laid up and have been designated as future fleet targets.

HMS Ledbury

MINE COUNTERMEASURES SHIPS (MCMV'S) HUNT CLASS

Ship	Pennant Number	Completion Date	Builder
BRECON	M29	1980	Vosper T.
LEDBURY	M30	1981	Vosper T.
CATTISTOCK	M31	1982	Vosper T.
COTTESMORE	M32	1983	Yarrow
BROCKLESBY	M33	1983	Vosper T.
MIDDLETON	M34	1984	Yarrow
DULVERTON	M35	1983	Vosper T.
CHIDDINGFOLD	M37	1984	Vosper T.
ATHERSTONE	M38	1987	Vosper T.
HURWORTH	M39	1985	Vosper T.
QUORN	M41	1989	Vosper T.

Displacement 625 tonnes **Dimensions** 60m x 10m x 2.2m **Speed** 17 knots **Armament** 1 x 30mm + 2 x 20mm guns **Complement** 42.

Notes

The largest warships ever built of glass reinforced plastic. Their cost (£35m each) has dictated the size of the class. Very sophisticated ships – and lively seaboats! All based at Portsmouth and Faslane. Ships are frequently deployed in the Fishery Protection role. COTTESMORE, BRECON and DULVERTON refitted as patrol boats for operations off Northern Ireland. Two of the class were sold to Greece in 2000 and 2001. BRECON is scheduled to decommission in 2016, BROCKLESBY, CHIDDINGFOLD, QUORN, HURWORTH, ATHERSTONE and DULVERTON in 2020, COTTESMORE 2022 and LEDBURY 2023.

HMS Pembroke

SANDOWN CLASS

Ship	Pennant Number	Completion Date	Builder
SANDOWN	M101	1989	Vosper T.
INVERNESS	M102	1991	Vosper T.
WALNEY	M104	1992	Vosper T.
BRIDPORT	M105	1993	Vosper T.
PENZANCE	M106	1998	Vosper T.
PEMBROKE	M107	1998	Vosper T.
GRIMSBY	M108	1999	Vosper T.
BANGOR	M109	2000	Vosper T.
RAMSEY	M110	2000	Vosper T.
BLYTH	M111	2001	Vosper T.
SHOREHAM	M112	2001	Vosper T.

Displacement 450 tons **Dimensions** 53m x 10m x 2m **Speed** 13 knots **Armament** 1 - 30mm gun **Complement** 34.

Notes
A class dedicated to a single mine hunting role. Propulsion is by vectored thrust and bow thrusters. CROMER paid off in 2001 and was towed to Dartmouth in 2002 to become a static training hull (renamed HINDUSTAN). After 18 months at Faslane in Extended Readiness BRIDPORT was towed to Portsmouth in Nov 03. Her future remains undecided.

HMS Dumbarton Castle

PATROL VESSELS
CASTLE CLASS

Ship	Pennant Number	Completion Date	Builder
LEEDS CASTLE	P258	1981	Hall Russell
DUMBARTON CASTLE	P265	1982	Hall Russell

Displacement 1,450 tons **Dimensions** 81m x 11m x 3m **Speed** 20 knots **Armament** 1 - 30mm gun **Complement** 42

Notes

These ships have a dual role – that of fishery protection and offshore patrols within the limits of UK territorial waters. Unlike the Island Class these ships are able to operate helicopters – including Sea King aircraft. LEEDS CASTLE is on long term deployment to the Falkland Islands with her ships' company rotating every four months. DUMBARTON CASTLE now has an MCM role. Vosper Thornycroft have submitted a proposal to MoD to replace these two ageing vessels with two further River class, modified to operate a helicopter.

HMS Tyne

RIVER CLASS

Ship	Pennant Number	Completion Date	Builder
TYNE	P281	2002	Vosper T.
SEVERN	P282	2003	Vosper T.
MERSEY	P283	2003	Vosper T.

Displacement 1700 tonnes **Dimensions** 80m x 13.5m x 3.8m **Speed** 20+ knots
Armament 1 x 20mm, 2 x GPMG **Complement** 48

Notes
Ordered on 8 May 2001, the deal is unusual in that the ships are being leased from
Vospers (VT) for five years under a £60 million contract. Thereafter the opportunity
exists for the lease to be extended, the ships purchased outright or returned to VT. The
contract also provides for VT to dispose of the Island class. ANGLESEY was trans-
ferred to Bangladesh in 2003 and renamed GOMATI. GUERNSEY and LINDES-
FARNE were due to be withdrawn from service in January 2004 and transferred to
Bangladesh being renamed TURAG and SANGU respectively.

HMS Scimitar

LIFESPAN PATROL VESSELS (LPVs)

Ship	Pennant Number	Completion Date	Builder
SCIMITAR	P284	1988	Halmatic
SABRE	P285	1988	Halmatic

Displacement 18.5 tons **Dimensions** 16m x 4.7m x 1.4m **Speed** 27+ knots
Armament Nil **Complement** 4

Notes

Purpose built in 1988 for counter terrorism duties on Lough Neagh, Northern Ireland. Operated in anonimity until withdrawn from service in 2002, following a review of RN operations in the Province. Transferred to Gibraltar in September 2002 to join the Gibraltar Patrol Boat Squadron. On completion of trials they were commissioned on 31 January 2003 and renamed SCIMITAR (ex-GREYFOX) and SABRE (ex-GREY-WOLF). They have replaced the P2000 patrol boats TRUMPETER and RANGER.

COASTAL TRAINING CRAFT
P2000 CLASS

Ship	Pennant Number	Completion Date	Builder
EXPRESS	P163	1988	Vosper T.
EXPLORER	P164	1985	Watercraft
EXAMPLE	P165	1985	Watercraft
EXPLOIT	P167	1988	Vosper T.
ARCHER	P264	1985	Watercraft
BITER	P270	1985	Watercraft
SMITER	P272	1986	Watercraft
PURSUER	P273	1988	Vosper T.
TRACKER	P274	1998	Ailsa Troon
RAIDER	P275	1998	Ailsa Troon
BLAZER	P279	1988	Vosper T.
DASHER	P280	1988	Vosper T.
PUNCHER	P291	1988	Vosper T.
CHARGER	P292	1988	Vosper T.
RANGER	P293	1988	Vosper T.
TRUMPETER	P294	1988	Vosper T.

Displacement 43 tonnes **Dimensions** 20m x 6m x 1m **Speed** 20 knots **Armament** 1 x GPMG (Gibraltar/Cyprus vessels) **Complement** 5 (with accommodation for up to 12 undergraduates).

Notes
In service with RN University units (URNU) as training vessels. TRUMPETER and RANGER deployed to Gibraltar in 1991 and armed in 2002. TRUMPETER returned to the UK in 2003 and RANGER is expected to follow in 2004. DASHER and PURSUER were transferred to Cyprus at the end of 2002 to form a new Cyprus Squadron to patrol the Sovereign Base Areas. Vessels are assigned to the following URNUs: ARCHER (Aberdeen); BITER (Manchester); BLAZER (Southampton); CHARGER (Liverpool); TRUMPETER (Bristol); EXAMPLE (Northumbria); EXPLOIT (Birmingham); EXPLORER (Yorkshire); EXPRESS (Wales); PUNCHER (London); RANGER (Sussex); RAIDER (Cambridge); SMITER (Glasgow); TRACKER (Oxford).

HMS Raider

HMS Example

HMS Scott

SURVEY SHIPS

Ship	Pennant Number	Completion Date	Builder
SCOTT	H 131	1997	Appledore

Displacement 13,300 tonnes **Dimensions** 130m x 21.5m x 14m **Speed** 17 knots **Complement** 63

Notes

SCOTT carries a mixture of the latest UK and US survey equipment. The sonar system is US supplied. She operates a three watch system whereby the vessel is run by 42 of the ships company of 63 with the remainder on leave. Each crew member works 75 days in the ship before having 30 days off, allowing her to spend more than 300 days at sea in a year. These manpower reductions over previous survey ships have been possible because of the extensive use of commercial lean manning methods including unmanned machinery spaces, fixed fire fighting systems and extensive machinery and safety surveillance technology.

28

HMS Enterprise

ECHO CLASS

Ship	Pennant Number	Completion Date	Builder
ECHO	H 87	2002	Appledore
ENTERPRISE	H 88	2003	Appledore

Displacement 3,470 tonnes **Dimensions** 90m x 16.8m x 5.5.m **Speed** 15 knots **Complement** 46 (with accommodation for 81)

Notes

In June 2000, a £130 million order was placed with prime contractor Vosper Thornycroft to build and maintain, over a 25 year period, two new Survey Vessels Hydrographic Oceanographic (SVHO). Both vessels were built by sub-contractor Appledore Shipbuilding Limited. They have a secondary role as mine countermeasures flag ships. ECHO entered service in 2003 and. ENTERPRISE was scheduled to follow by early 2004. They will be operationally available for 330 days a year. Utilizing a diesel electric propulsion system, they have three main generators. They are the first RN ships to be fitted with Azimuth pod thrusters in place of the more normal shaft and propellor. Problems with the pods saw ECHO laid up for a period in 2003 at Falmouth. ENTERPRISE had her pods removed at Portsmouth for transfer to ECHO. ENTERPRISE was towed to Plymouth in October 2003 where she commissioned on the 17th. She was to continue training and work-up alongside until new pods become available.

HMS Roebuck

Ship	Pennant Number	Completion Date	Builder
ROEBUCK	H130	1986	Brooke Marine

Displacement 1500 tonnes **Dimensions** 64m x 13m x 4m **Speed** 15 knots **Complement** 51.

Notes

Able to operate for long periods away from shore support, this ship and the other vessels of the Hydrographic Fleet collect the data that is required to produce the Admiralty Charts and publications which are sold to mariners worldwide. Fitted with the latest fixing aids and sector scanning sonar. Was scheduled to pay-off in April 2003 but following operations during the Iraq war she has been extended in service until 2014.

HMS Gleaner

INSHORE SURVEY VESSEL

Ship	Pennant Number	Completion Date	Builder
GLEANER	H86	1983	Emsworth

Displacement 22 tons **Dimensions** 14.8m x 4.7m x 1.3m **Speed** 14 knots **Complement** 5.

Notes
Small inshore survey craft used for the collection of data from the shallowest inshore waters. Will remain in service until at least 2007.

HMS Endurance

ICE PATROL SHIP

Ship	Pennant Number	Completion Date	Builder
ENDURANCE	A171	1990	Ulstein-Hatlo

Displacement 5,129 tons **Dimensions** 91m x 17.9m x 6.5m **Speed** 14.9 knots **Armament** Small arms **Aircraft** 2 Lynx **Complement** 116

Notes
Chartered for only 7 months in late 1991 to replace the older vessel of the same name. Originally M/V POLAR CIRCLE, renamed HMS POLAR CIRCLE (A176) and then purchased by MOD(N) and renamed again in October 1992 to current name. Spends 4-6 months each year in the South Atlantic supporting the British Antarctic Survey. Will remain in service until at least 2015.

Griffon 2000 TDX (M)

ROYAL MARINE CRAFT
4 GRIFFON 2000 TDX (M) LCAC

Pennants C21 - C24 **G.R.T.** 6.8 tons **Dimensions** 12m x 5m **Speed** 33 knots

Armament 1 x GPMG **Complement** 2

Notes
Ordered in April 1993, these four lightly armoured Landing Craft Air Cushion (LCAC) are operated by 539 Assault Squadron. Used extensively during the Iraq War to patrol the marshlands and waterways around Basra. They have the capacity to lift 12 fully equipped troops or 2 x 1000kg pallets of stores and are capable of deployment in C-130 Hercules transport aircraft. It is expected that the current fleet of hovercraft will be replaced in around 2007.

SPECIALIST CRAFT

In addition to the familiar Rigid Raiding Craft and Rigid Inflatable Boats the Royal Marines also operate a range of specialist craft for more covert and special operations which can deploy from both ships and submarines. Air transportable Fast Insertion Craft (FIC) with a speed of 55 knots are known to be in service as are advanced wave piercing designs.
Swimmer Delivery Vehicles (SDV), in reality miniature submarines, which can be deployed from dry deck shelters on larger submarines, are also a part of the UK Special Forces inventory.

LCU Mk10

10 LCU Mk10

Pennants L1001 - L1010 **G.R.T.** 240 tons FL **Dimensions** 29.8m x 7.4m x 1.7m **Speed** 8.5 knots **Complement** 7.

Notes
Ro-Ro style landing craft designed to operate from the Albion class LPDs. Ordered in 1998 from Ailsa Troon. The first two were delivered in 1999. The remainder were built by BAE Systems at Govan. Capable of lifting one Main Battle Tank or four lighter vehicles. Capacity for 120 troops. Several older LCU Mk9s remain in service and saw service in Kuwait during the recent Iraq War.

23 LCVP Mk5

Pennants 9473, 9673-9692, 9707, 9708 **G.R.T.** 25 tons FL **Dimensions** 15m x 4m x 1.5m **Speed** 20 knots **Complement** 3.

Notes
First one ordered in 1995 from Vosper Thornycroft and handed over in 1996. A further four were delivered in December 1996 to operate from OCEAN, with two more for RM Poole ordered in 1998. A further 16 were ordered from Babcock in 2001. The Mk 5 can lift 8 tonnes of stores or a mix of 2 tonnes and 35 troops. These vessels have a greater range, lift and speed than the Mk 4s which they are gradually replacing.

SHIPS FOR THE FUTURE FLEET...

ASTUTE - The Astute Class will be the Navy's replacement for the S Class nuclear powered fleet submarines. The contract for ASTUTE, AMBUSH and ARTFUL was placed in March 1997. Early in 2003, the programme ran into considerable difficulties, the result of which was that the contract was re-negotiated. The In Service Date (ISD) for ASTUTE is now 2008. She is unlikely to become fully operational until 2009. AMBUSH was laid down in October 2003. Revised ISDs for Nos. 2 and 3 have not been disclosed. A second batch of three submarines has been postponed indefinitely.

TYPE 45 - Although "up to" twelve ships are planned only six are presently on order. The next batch is not due to be ordered until later this decade. DARING (first of class) will be constructed at Scotstoun on the Clyde. All remaining ships will now be assembled and launched on the Clyde, as opposed to at Barrow. Construction will involve prefabricated methods and be divided between BAE and VT (Vosper Thornycroft). The ISD for DARING is scheduled for November 2007. The remaining five ships will follow between 2009 and 2011. It is planned that their availability will be 70% for 25 years. The PAAMS surface to air system will enable the ship to take out eight incoming missiles simultaneously. It has been announced that Ultra - MFS 7000 Sonar will be fitted to the first of class and not be fitted retrospectively after construction. The 2003 National Audit Office Report disclosed that the programme would cost £5.3 billion if no more ships were ordered. If another six ships are ordered, the overall cost will be £9 billion. Unit production cost is put at £633 million. Work on DARING commenced in June 2003.

FUTURE CARRIER PROGRAMME (CVF) - In January 2003, much to everyone's surprise, the Government failed to select as prime contractor for the CVF programme either Thales-UK or BAE SYSTEMS. Instead, the MOD decided on a joint programme. Since then, many questions have been raised over the feasibility of such a programme. The Commons Defence Committee has reported that this will create very difficult issues which could defeat the MOD. In June 2003, BAE approached the Government for more money, because the programme is now likely to cost £4 billion as opposed to £2.8 billion.

The Government will announce a demonstration and manufacturing contract for the new carriers in the spring of 2004. Construction is likely to be prefabricated mega-blocks with final assembly at Rosyth.

MILITARY AFLOAT REACH AND SUSTAINABILITY (MARS) - The MARS Integrated Project Team (IPT) is conducting studies into the capability required to provide logistic support to RN vessels at sea. The initial focus will be on the ability to Replenish At Sea with fuel, oil and lubricants, fresh water, food and ammunition. It was anticipated that the project would progress to its Assessment phase before the end of 2003. During this phase the project team will invite industry to provide solutions to this requirement, including ship designs, and will establish how new technologies and logistics concepts can deliver the increases in flexibility and responsiveness our future forces will require. Vessels to be replaced under the MARS project include the Rover, Leaf and Fort I classes.

JOINT CASUALTY TREATMENT SHIP (JCTS) - Originally known as the 'Primary Casualty Receiving Ship' (PCRS), and announced in the SDR was renamed in April 03 to become the JCTS (Joint Casualty Treatment Ship). The JCTS differs from a hospital ship in that it operates as part of a maritime task force, and is not subject to the kinds of restrictions that the Geneva Conventions place on a white-painted, red-cross, hospital ship. The JCTS is expected to include up to 8 operating tables and not less than 150 beds, together with the full range of intensive care and other facilities that one would expect to find in a shore-based public hospital. The work carried out to date has indicated that a new vessel, based upon a proven commercial hull design, should produce the best value for money solution to the requirement. A contract was let in July 2003 for the completion of a System Requirement Document. Current plans envisage the issue of Invitations to Tender for the design and construction of the ship around the end of the 2004/5 financial year.

THE ROYAL FLEET AUXILIARY

The Royal Fleet Auxiliary Service (RFA) is a civilian manned fleet owned and operated by the Ministry of Defence. Its main task is to supply warships of the Royal Navy at sea with fuel, food, stores and ammunition which they need to remain operational while away from base.The service also provides aviation support and training facilities for the Royal Navy – together with amphibious support and secure sea transport for for the Royal Marines and British Army units.

The RFA is the largest single employer of UK merchant navy officers and ratings. Although the ethos is very much based on that of the Merchant Service, the personnel undergo a considerable overlay of naval training, in the main to provide them with a greater degree of survivability when operating their ships in hostile waters. Such training includes the operation and maintenance of close range and small calibre weapons and decoys (self-defence weapons), firefighting and damage control. But, fundamental to the success of the RFA is the need for competent seamen to undertake replenishment at sea and small boat operations, and to man ships flight decks to ensure the safe operation of helicopters.

The service prides itself that each ship is available for operations for approximately 80% of the year and as 2003 arrived the RFA fleet found itself preparing to commit the majority of its vessels to support a possible war in the Gulf region. Ships that were preparing to deploy on a routine Far East deployment were redeployed to the Gulf to support a much enlarged Task Force. At the start of 2003 the RFA fleet comprised 18 operational vessels, with two new Wave class working up prior to acceptance. By February all but one of the fleet was deployed. BLACK ROVER was deployed to the West Indies, GREY ROVER was in the South Atlantic and GOLD ROVER was acting as FOST tanker at Devonport. BAYLEAF and SIR BEDIVERE were already operating in the Gulf and DILIGENCE was heading there from submarine support operations in the Far East. Of the remaining twelve vessels in the fleet all, bar one were deployed in support of Gulf operations. The only ship left out was FORT GEORGE which was preparing to enter refit.

While the Royal Navy gradually replaces old tonnage, the RFA has for many years soldiered on with vessels which it can be argued are long in the tooth, the oldest LSLs first entered service in 1967, the Rover class tankers in the 1970s, Fort I class in the late 1970's and the Leaf class in 1980-82. However, new tonnage is on the way. The two Wave class tankers have now entered service, and indeed WAVE KNIGHT deployed for the first time in the summer of 2003 to support the Atlantic Patrol Ship (North). The first of the new and potentially highly capable Bay class Landing Ship Dock (Auxiliary)s, LARGS BAY is expected to be completed in 2004 to begin replacing the LSLs. Although only four ships are to be acquired they represent a quantum leap in capability over their predecessors.

Of concern are the number of vessels that are scheduled to pay off before the end of the decade, for which there appears to be no replacement. The Military Afloat Reach and Sustainability (MARS) project has reached its assessment phase but it is not known whether it will be able to deliver replacement hulls for the Leaf, Rover and Fort I classes before the first of these ships goes out of service in 2007. The urgency for their replacements is all the more pressing following new international regulations governing the operation of single hull tankers, into which catergory these three classes fall. More worrying though is the declared departure of DILIGENCE in 2006 and ARGUS in 2008, both vessels which provide a unique service and for which there is currently no programme in situ to replace them.

One constant however, remains. As long as the Royal Navy goes to sea, the demand for RFA support remains. As the RN tempo of operations remains high around the world, the RFA will continue to provide support wherever it is needed with those vessels available. For the immediate future it appears that the RFA will be busier than ever.

SHIPS OF THE ROYAL FLEET AUXILIARY
Pennant Numbers

Ship	Pennant Number	Ship	Pennant Number	Ship	Pennant Number
BRAMBLELEAF	A81	BLACK ROVER	A273	SIR GALAHAD	L3005
BAYLEAF	A109	FORT ROSALIE	A385	LARGS BAY	L3006
ORANGELEAF	A110	FORT AUSTIN	A386	LYME BAY	L3007
OAKLEAF	A111	FORT VICTORIA	A387	MOUNTS BAY	L3008
DILIGENCE	A132	FORT GEORGE	A388	CARDIGAN BAY	L3009
ARGUS	A135	WAVE KNIGHT	A389	SIR PERCIVALE	L3036
GREY ROVER	A269	WAVE RULER	A390	SIR TRISTRAM	L3505
GOLD ROVER	A271	SIR BEDIVERE	L3004		

KEEP UP TO DATE
THROUGHOUT THE YEAR

Warship World is published six times a year (Jan, Mar, May, Jul, Sep, Nov) and gives you all the information necessary to keep this book updated throughout the year. Now in full colour.

RFA Wave Knight

FLEET TANKERS
WAVE CLASS

Ship	Pennant Number	Completion Date	Builder
WAVE KNIGHT	A 389	2002	BAE SYSTEMS
WAVE RULER	A 390	2002	BAE SYSTEMS

Displacement 30,300 tons (Full Load) **Dimensions** 196 x 27 x 10m **Speed** 18 knots
Armament 2 x Vulcan Phalanx (fitted for but not with), 2 x 30mm **Aircraft** 1 Merlin
Complement 80 (plus 22 Fleet Air Arm)

Notes
A new class of Fast Fleet Support Tankers to replace the two O class vessels sold for scrap in 2000. WAVE KNIGHT was handed over from the builders at the end of September 2002 and accepted into service in March 2003. WAVE RULER was launched in February 2001 at Govan, and was handed over from the builders in October 2002. She accepted into service in April 2003. The ships have a cargo capacity of 16,900 tonnes (Fuel) and 915 tonnes (Dry Stores).

RFA Oakleaf

SUPPORT TANKERS

Ship	Pennant Number	Completion Date	Builder
OAKLEAF	A111	1981	Uddevalla

Displacement 49,310 tons **Dimensions** 173.7m x 32.2m x 11.2m **Speed** 14 knots **Complement** 35.

Notes

At 49,310 tons displacement, she is the largest vessel in RN/RFA service. Her role, along with other support tankers, is to provide the fuel vital to enable the Navy's warships to operate far from their UK bases. Scheduled to decommission in 2015.

• MARITIME PHOTOGRAPHIC

RFA Brambleleaf

LEAF CLASS

Ship	Pennant Number	Completion Date	Builder
BRAMBLELEAF	A81	1980	Cammell Laird
BAYLEAF	A109	1982	Cammell Laird
ORANGELEAF	A110	1982	Cammell Laird

Displacement 37,747 tons **Dimensions** 170m x 26m x 12m **Speed** 14.5 knots **Complement** 60.

Notes

All are ex-merchant ships, originally acquired for employment mainly on freighting duties. All have been modified to enable them to refuel warships at sea. BRAMBLE-LEAF is MoD(N) owned, the remainder on long-term bareboat charter. All are commercial Stat32 class tankers. ORANGELEAF is to decommission in 2008 and the remaining two in 2009.

The MoD also has the commercial tanker MAERSK RAPIER on permanent charter. She is a multi-tasked tanker which supplies all fuel to the naval facilities in the UK, Gibraltar, the Falkland Islands and Souda Bay, Crete. She is also chartered to supply aviation fuel to Cyprus, Ascension Island and the Falkland Islands. The MoD charters the vessel to commercial companies when it is not in use for defence requirements.

RFA Gold Rover

ROVER CLASS

Ship	Pennant Number	Completion Date	Builder
GREY ROVER	A269	1970	Swan Hunter
GOLD ROVER	A271	1974	Swan Hunter
BLACK ROVER	A273	1974	Swan Hunter

Displacement 11,522 tons **Dimensions** 141m x 19m x 7m **Speed** 18 knots **Armament** 2 - 20mm guns **Complement** 49/54

Notes

Small Fleet Tankers designed to supply warships with fresh water, dry cargo and refrigerated provisions, as well as a range of fuels and lubricants. Helicopter deck, but no hangar. Have been employed in recent years mainly as support for HM Ships operating around the Falkland Islands and West Indies, spending up to two years on deployment in these areas. All three ships are scheduled to decommission in 2007.

RFA Fort Austin

STORES VESSELS
FORT CLASS I

Ship	Pennant Number	Completion Date	Builder
FORT ROSALIE	A385	1978	Scott Lithgow
FORT AUSTIN	A386	1979	Scott Lithgow

Displacement 23,384 tons **Dimensions** 183m x 24m x 9m **Speed** 20 knots
Complement 201, (120 RFA, 36 MoD Civilians & 45 Fleet Air Arm).

Notes
Full hangar and maintenance facilities are provided and up to four Sea King helicopters
can be carried for both the transfer of stores and anti-submarine protection of a group
of ships. Both ships can be armed with 4 - 20mm guns. FORT ROSALIE is to decommission in 2013 and FORT AUSTIN in 2014.

RFA Fort George

REPLENISHMENT SHIPS
FORT CLASS II

Ship	Pennant Number	Completion Date	Builder
FORT VICTORIA	A387	1992	Harland & Wolff
FORT GEORGE	A388	1993	Swan Hunter

Displacement 31,500 tons **Dimensions** 204m x 30m x 9m **Speed** 20 knots **Armament** 4 - 30mm guns, 2 x Phalanx CIWS, Sea Wolf Missile System (Fitted for but not with) **Complement** 100 (RFA), 24 MoD Civilians, 32 RN and up to 122 Fleet Air Arm.

Notes
"One stop" replenishment ships with the widest range of armaments, fuel and spares carried. Can operate up to 5 Sea King/ 3 Merlin Helicopters (more in a ferry role) with full maintenance facilities onboard. Medical facilities were upgraded with a 12 bed surgical capability in 2001 to give the vessels a limited role as Primary Casualty Receiving Ships. Both are to remain in service until 2019.

RFA Sir Bedivere

LANDING SHIPS (LOGISTIC)
SIR CLASS

Ship	Pennant Number	Completion Date	Builder
SIR BEDIVERE	L3004	1967	Hawthorn
SIR GALAHAD	L3005	1987	Swan Hunter
SIR PERCIVALE	L3036	1968	Hawthorn
SIR TRISTRAM	L3505	1967	Hawthorn

Displacement 5,550 tons **Dimensions** 126m x 18m x 4m **Speed** 17 knots **Armament** Can be fitted with 20 or 40mm guns in emergency **Complement** 65, (SIR GALAHAD is larger at 8,451 tons. 140m x 20m **Complement** 58)

Notes

Manned by the RFA but tasked by the Commodore Amphibious Task Group (COMATG), these ships are used for heavy secure transport of stores – embarked by bow and stern doors. Can operate helicopters from both vehicle and flight deck if required and carry 340 troops. SIR TRISTRAM was rebuilt after extensive Falklands War damage. After extensive delays, SIR BEDIVERE completed a Ship Life Extension Programme (SLEP) at Rosyth in 1998. She is now 7,700 tonnes displacement and her dimensions are 137 x 20 x 4 metres. Occasionally used for MCMV support. SIR GERAINT paid off in 2003. SIR TRISTRAM is to pay off in 2005, SIR GALAHAD and SIR PERCIVALE in 2006. SIR BEDIVERE is likely to continue in service.

RFA Largs Bay

LANDING SHIP DOCK (AUXILIARY) BAY CLASS

Ship	Pennant Number	Completion Date	Builder
LARGS BAY	L3006	2004	Swan Hunter
LYME BAY	L3007	Building	Swan Hunter
MOUNTS BAY	L3008	Building	BAE SYSTEMS
CARDIGAN BAY	L3009	Building	BAE SYSTEMS

Displacement 16,190 tonnes **Dimensions** 176.6m x 26.4m x 5.1m **Speed** 18 knots **Armament** Fitted to receive in emergency **Complement** 60

Notes: The design and build contract for two vessels was signed with Swan Hunter in December 2000. A further two vessels were ordered from BAE Systems in November 2001. In 2002 the vessels were designated LSD(A) to meet NATO disignation requirements for a vessel that has an integral dock. The dock is capable of operating LCU 10s and they carry two LCVP Mk5s. They can offload at sea, over the horizon. In addition to their war fighting role they are well suited to disaster relief and other humanitarian missions.

RFA Diligence

FORWARD REPAIR SHIP

Ship	Pennant Number	Completion Date	Builder
DILIGENCE	A132	1981	Oesundsvarvet

Displacement 5,814 tons **Dimensions** 120m x 12m x 3m **Speed** 15 knots **Armament** 2 - 20mm **Complement** RFA 40, RN Personnel – approx 100.

Notes

Formerly the M/V Stena Inspector purchased (£25m) for service in the South Atlantic. Her deep diving complex was removed and workshops added. When not employed on "battle repair" duties can serve as support vessel for MCMVs and submarines on deployment. Scheduled to decommission in 2006. A probable replacement will be required, the likely earliest date for such being 2010. It remains a possibility that the current ship will remain in service until then.

RFA Argus

AVIATION TRAINING SHIP

Ship	Pennant Number	Completion Date	Builder
ARGUS	A135	1981	Cantieri Navali Breda

Displacement 28,081 tons (full load) **Dimensions** 175m x 30m x 8m **Speed** 18 knots
Armament 4 - 30 mm, 2 - 20 mm **Complement** 254 (inc 137 Fleet Air Arm)
Aircraft 6 Sea King/Merlin, 12 Harriers can be carried in a "ferry role".

Notes

Formerly the M/V CONTENDER BEZANT taken up from trade during the Falklands crisis. Purchased in 1984 (£13 million) for conversion to an 'Aviation Training Ship'. A £50 million re-build was undertaken at Belfast from 1984-87. Undertook rapid conversion in October 1990 to Primary Casualty Reception Ship for service in the Gulf. These facilities were upgraded and made permanent during 2001. Scheduled to decommission in 2008. A replacement for the Aviation Ship and PCRS role is currently under review. A new RFA PCRS is almost certain, but probaly not in dual role as an Aviation ship and PCRS. If a new purpose-built/adapted ship is not acquired a likely scenario is that other RFAs with deck/hangar facilities are used for aviation training (as is the case now when ARGUS is unavailable) or the task may be carried out on RN decks.

MV Hurst Point

STRATEGIC SEALIFT RO-RO VESSELS

Ship	Pennant Number	Completion Date	Builder
HURST POINT		2002	Flensburger
HARTLAND POINT		2002	Harland & Wolff
EDDYSTONE		2002	Flensburger
LONGSTONE		2003	Flensburger
ANVIL POINT		2003	Harland & Wolff
BEACHY HEAD		2003	Flensburger

Displacement 10,000 tonnes, 13,300 tonnes (FL) **Dimensions** 193m x 26m x 6.6m **Speed** 18 knots **Complement** 38

Notes
The contract for the supply of six ro-ro vessels to meet the requirements for stategic sealift capabilities was announced in October 2000. Under a 25 year private finance initiative deal, AWSR Shipping Limited were contracted to build and run the vessels for the MoD. The contract, likely to be worth up to £950 million, was finally signed on 27 June 2002. The MoD will normally use four of the ships, with all six available for operations. The unarmed ships have green hulls, white superstructure, yellow funnels and fly the Red Ensign. BEACHY HEAD and LONGSTONE are on charter to the Finnish company Transfennica Limited. RFA SEA CRUSADER was returned to her owners in 2003.

HMS ALBION

HMS INVINCIBLE MoD/Crown Copyright

HMS CHATHAM

F87

MoD/Crown Copyright

HMS CHATHAM

F87

MoD/Crown Copyright

HMS ENDURANCE (Right) WITH RRS ERNEST SHACKLETON

MoD/Crown Copyright

HMS MARLBOROUGH

MoD/Crown Copyright

HMS SPARTAN

Dave Cullen

MoD/Crown Copyright

RFA SIR GALAHAD DELIVERING AID TO IRAQ

MARINE SERVICES SUPPORT

The Chief Executive Warship Support Agency (WSA) is tasked by the Defence Logistic Organisation (DLO) with Tri-Service provision of Marine Services and is responsible for In and Out-of-Port maritime services in support of Naval Bases, CinC Fleet, The Meteorological Office, QinetiQ (formerly DERA), RAF and Army. Their role is to undertake Mooring and Navigation buoy maintenance, freighting of Naval armaments and explosives, maritime support to the underwater research programme and sea-borne services to the Fleet. Maritime services at the Kyle of Lochalsh are provided primarily to support the BUTEC Ranges, and secondarily to fulfil Fleet requirements in that area.

In the three main ports at Portsmouth, Devonport and Clyde the service is currently delivered under a Government Owned/Commercially Operated (GOCO) contract with SERCo-Denholm Ltd. The vessels being operated on a BARECON (Bareboat charter) basis. The contract is due to be re-let in October 2005.

For Naval Armament Freighting, Mooring Maintenance, RMAS NEWTON and services at Kyle of Lochalsh, the service is currently delivered by the General Manager RMAS from his HQ at Pembroke Dock.

A 10-year PPP/PFI contract with an effective date of 1 April 2002 was placed with Smit International (Scotland) Ltd to carry out Marine Support to Ranges and Air Crew Training. Since that date Smit have replaced all the MoD craft with a fleet of new and second hand tonnage.

Marine Services vessels can be seen at work in the UK Naval Bases and are easily identified by their black hulls, buff coloured superstructure and by their Flag, which in the case of GM RMAS vessels, is a blue ensign defaced in the fly by a yellow anchor over two wavy lines. The remaining vessels fly the 'Other Government' ensign. Which is a blue ensign defaced in the fly by a yellow anchor.

SHIPS OF
THE MARINE SERVICES
Pennant Numbers

Ship	Pennant Number	Page	Ship	Pennant Number	Page
CAMERON	A72	77	ADEPT	A224	60
MELTON	A83	72	BUSTLER	A225	60
MENAI	A84	72	CAPABLE	A226	60
MEON	A87	72	CAREFUL	A227	60
TORNADO	A140	75	FAITHFUL	A228	60
TORMENTOR	A142	75	COL. TEMPLER	A229	65
WATERMAN	A146	75	DEXTEROUS	A231	60
FRANCES	A147	63	ADAMANT	A232	71
FLORENCE	A149	63	NEWHAVEN	A280	68
GENEVIEVE	A150	63	NUTBOURNE	A281	68
LESLEY	A172	62	NETLEY	A282	68
HUSKY	A178	61	OBAN	A283	69
SALUKI	A182	61	ORONSAY	A284	69
SALMOOR	A185	76	OMAGH	A285	69
SALMAID	A187	76	PADSTOW	A286	70
BOVISAND	A191	67	IMPULSE	A344	59
CAWSAND	A192	67	IMPETUS	A345	59
HELEN	A198	63	NEWTON	A367	64
MYRTLE	A199	62	WARDEN	A368	78
SPANIEL	A201	61	KINTERBURY	A378	66
FORCEFUL	A221	60	OILPRESS	Y21	73
NIMBLE	A222	60	MOORHEN	Y32	77
POWERFUL	A223	60	MOORFOWL	Y33	77

MV Impetus

TUGS

IMPULSE CLASS

Ship	Pennant Number	Completion Date	Builder
IMPULSE	A344	1993	R. Dunston
IMPETUS	A345	1993	R. Dunston

G.R.T. 400 tons approx **Dimensions** 33m x 10m x 4m **Speed** 12 knots **Complement** 5.

Notes
Completed in 1993 specifically to serve as berthing tugs for the Trident Class submarines at Faslane. Both operated under contract by Serco Denholm.

MV Powerful

TWIN UNIT TRACTOR TUGS (TUTT'S)

Ship	Pennant Number	Completion Date	Builder
FORCEFUL	A221	1985	R. Dunston
NIMBLE	A222	1985	R. Dunston
POWERFUL	A223	1985	R. Dunston
ADEPT	A224	1980	R. Dunston
BUSTLER	A225	1981	R. Dunston
CAPABLE	A226	1981	R. Dunston
CAREFUL	A227	1982	R. Dunston
FAITHFUL	A228	1985	R. Dunston
DEXTEROUS	A231	1986	R. Dunston

G.R.T. 375 tons **Dimensions** 39m x 10m x 4m **Speed** 12 knots **Complement** 9.

Notes

The principal harbour tugs in naval service. All operated under contract by Serco Denholm except CAPABLE at Gibraltar which is managed locally.

MV Saluki

DOG CLASS

Ship	Pennant Number	Completion Date	Builder
HUSKY	A178	1969	Appledore
SALUKI	A182	1969	Appledore
SPANIEL	A201	1967	Appledore

G.R.T. 152 tons **Dimensions** 29m x 8m x 4m **Speed** 12 knots **Complement** 5.

Notes

General harbour tugs – all completed between 1965 and 1969. COLLIE and CAIRN replaced at Kyle of Lochalsh by civilian vessels under charter to MoD during 2001. MASTIFF sold for commercial service. DALMATION withdrawn November 2003. SHEEPDOG and SETTER will be withdrawn early in 2004. The latter three (Portsmouth based) vessels will be replaced by contractors own craft.

MV Lesley

TRITON CLASS

Ship	Pennant Number	Completion Date	Builder
LESLEY	A172	1973	R. Dunston
MYRTLE	A199	1973	R. Dunston

G.R.T. 89 tons **Speed** 8 knots **Complement** 4.

Notes
Known as Water Tractors these craft are used for basin moves and towage of light barges. Operated by Serco Denholm Ltd. LILAH sold 2001. JOAN and NORAH were withdrawn in March and May 2003 respectively and are awaiting a buyer. KITTY was withdrawn at the end of 2003.

MV Genevieve

FELICITY CLASS

Ship	Pennant Number	Completion Date	Builder
FLORENCE	A149	1980	R. Dunston
FRANCES	A147	1980	R. Dunston
GENEVIEVE	A150	1980	R. Dunston
HELEN	A198	1974	R. Dunston

G.R.T. 80 tons **Speed** 10 knots **Complement** 4.

Notes

Water Tractors used for the movement of small barges and equipment. All are operated by Serco Denholm. Two sister vessels (GEORGINA and GWENDOLINE) sold to Serco Denholm in 1996 for service in H M Naval bases. FIONA for sale in 2003.

RMAS Newton

RESEARCH VESSELS

Ship	Pennant Number	Completion Date	Builder
NEWTON	A367	1976	Scotts

G.R.T. 2,779 tons **Dimensions** 99m x 16m x 6m **Speed** 15 knots **Complement** 27

Notes

Primarily used in the support of RN training exercises. Some limited support provided for various trials. Operated by the RMAS. Completed major refit in 2001 to extend life. Is frequently seen with Royal Marine small craft embarked.

MV Colonel Templer

Ship	Pennant Number	Completion Date	Builder
COLONEL TEMPLER A 229		1966	Hall Russell

Displacement 1,300 tons **Dimensions** 56m x 11m x 5.6 m **Speed** 12 knots
Complement 14

Notes

Built as a stern trawler but converted in 1980 for use by the Defence Evaluation and Research Agency as an acoustic research vessel. A major rebuild was completed after a serious fire gutted the ship in 1990. 12 scientists can be carried. From Nov 2000 operated on the Clyde by Serco Denholm. Used in support of trials and converted in 2001 to support RN diving training vice IXWORTH and IRONBRIDGE.

RMAS Kinterbury

NAVAL ARMAMENT VESSELS

Ship	Pennant Number	Completion Date	Builder
KINTERBURY	A378	1981	Appledore SB

G.R.T. 1,357 tons **Dimensions** 64m x 12m x 5m **Speed** 14 knots **Complement** 11.

Notes
Two holds carry Naval armament stores, ammunition and guided missiles. In addition to freighting tasks it is also used for trials work and in support of RN exercises. LADY-BIRD, the last of the 100ft Fleet Tenders/Armament Carriers, was laid up in 2003 and is awaiting disposal.

MV Cawsand

TENDERS
STORM CLASS

Ship	Pennant Number	Completion Date	Builder
BOVISAND	A191	1997	FBM (Cowes)
CAWSAND	A192	1997	FBM (Cowes)

G.R.T 225 tonnes **Dimensions** 23m x 11m x 2m **Speed** 15 knots **Complement** 5

Notes

These craft are used in support of Flag Officer Sea Training (FOST) at Plymouth to transfer staff quickly and comfortably to and from Warships and Auxiliaries within and beyond the Plymouth breakwater in open sea conditions. These are the first vessels of a small waterplane area twin hull (SWATH) design to be ordered by the Ministry of Defence and cost £6.5 million each. Speed restrictions implemented due to wash problems.

MV Nutbourne

NEWHAVEN CLASS

Ship	Pennant Number	Completion Date	Builder
NEWHAVEN	A280	2000	Aluminium SB
NUTBOURNE	A281	2000	Aluminium SB
NETLEY	A282	2001	Aluminium SB

Tonnage 77 tonnes (45 grt) **Dimensions** 18.3m x 6.8m x 1.88m **Speed** 10 knots **Complement** 3 Crew (60 passengers).

Notes
MCA Class IV Passenger Vessels based at Portsmouth. Replacements for Fleet tenders. Employed on general passenger duties.

• DONALD DONALDSON   **MV Oransay**

OBAN CLASS

Ship	Pennant Number	Completion Date	Builder
OBAN	A283	2000	McTay
ORONSAY	A284	2000	McTay
OMAGH	A285	2000	McTay

Tonnage 199 tons **Dimensions** 27.7m x 7.30m x 3.75m **Speed** 10 knots **Complement** 5 Crew (60 passengers).

Notes
 New MCA Class IIA Passenger Vessels to replace Fleet tenders. OBAN was transferred to Devonport in 2003 for use in supporting passenger transfers (other than FOST) and duties previously undertaken by LADYBIRD. ORANSAY and OMAGH employed on general passenger duties on the Clyde.

MV Padstow

PADSTOW CLASS

Ship	Pennant Number	Completion Date	Builder
PADSTOW	A286	2000	Aluminium SB

Tonnage 77 tonnes (45 grt) **Dimensions** 18.3m x 6.8m x 1.88m **Speed** 10 knots **Complement** 3 Crew (60 passengers).

Notes
MCA Class VIA Passenger Vessel based at Plymouth. Used on general passenger ferrying duties and in support of FOST staff.

• DONALD DONALDSON

MV Adamant

PERSONNEL FERRY

Ship	Pennant Number	Completion Date	Builder
ADAMANT	A232	1992	FBM (Cowes)

G.R.T 170 tonnes **Dimensions** 30m x 8m x 1m **Speed** 22 knots **Complement** 5

Notes
Twin catamaran hulls based on the commercial Red Jet design (as used by Red Funnel Ferry Co). First water jet propulsion vessel owned by MoD(N). In service as a Clyde personnel ferry - operated by Serco Denholm.

MV Menai

FLEET TENDERS

Ship	Pennant Number	Completion Date	Builder
MELTON	A83	1981	Richard Dunston
MENAI	A84	1981	Richard Dunston
MEON	A87	1982	Richard Dunston

G.R.T. 78 tons **Dimensions** 24m x 6m x 3m **Speed** 10.5 knots **Complement** 4/5.

Notes

The last three survivors of a once numerous class of tender used as Training Tenders, Passenger Ferries, or Cargo Vessels. MENAI and MEON are operated by Serco Denholm at Falmouth. MELTON is operated by the RMAS in Kyle. IRONBRIDGE, INSTOW, ILCHESTER and IXWORTH were withdrawn from service in November 2002, and have either been sold or are awaiting a buyer.

• DONALD DONALDSON

MV Oilpress

COASTAL OILER

Ship	Pennant Number	Completion Date	Builder
OILPRESS	Y21	1969	Appledore Shipbuilders

G.R.T. 362 tons **Dimensions** 41m x 9m x 3m **Speed** 11 knots **Complement** 5.

Notes
Employed as Harbour and Coastal Oiler. Operated by Serco Denholm on the Clyde.

MV Waterman

WATER CARRIER

Ship	Pennant Number	Completion Date	Builder
WATERMAN	A146	1978	R. Dunston

G.R.T. 263 tons **Dimensions** 40m x 8m x 2m **Speed** 11 knots **Complement** 5.

Notes
Capable of coastal passages, but normally supplies either demineralised or fresh water to the Fleet within port limits. WATERFOWL is owned and operated by Serco Denholm.

MV Tormentor

TORPEDO RECOVERY VESSELS (TRV)
TORNADO CLASS

Ship	Pennant Number	Completion Date	Builder
TORNADO	A140	1979	Hall Russell
TORMENTOR	A142	1980	Hall Russell

G.R.T. 560 tons **Dimensions** 47m x 8m x 3m **Speed** 14 knots **Complement** 13.

Notes
All vessels have had suitable rails fitted to enable them to operate as exercise minelay-ers. Converted in 2002 to support RN diving training (in lieu of Fleet Tenders) in addition to their other roles.

RMAS Salmaid

MOORING & SALVAGE VESSELS
SAL CLASS

Ship	Pennant Number	Completion Date	Builder
SALMOOR	A185	1985	Hall Russell
SALMAID	A187	1986	Hall Russell

Displacement 2,200 tonnes **Dimensions** 77m x 15m x 4m **Speed** 15 knots **Complement** 19

Notes
Multi-purpose vessels designed to lay and maintain underwater targets, navigation marks and moorings.

MV Moorhen

MOOR CLASS

Ship	Pennant Number	Completion Date	Builder
MOORHEN	Y32	1989	McTay Marine
MOORFOWL	Y33	1989	McTay Marine
CAMERON	A72	1991	Richard Dunston

Displacement 518 tons **Dimensions** 32m x 11m x 2m **Speed** 8 knots **Complement** 10

Notes

Powered mooring lighters for use within sheltered coastal waters. CAMERON is similar but was sold to DERA at Dunfermline in 1996 and is employed as an Underwater Trials & Experimental vessel at Rosyth. Operated by Briggs Marine on behalf of QinetiQ. MOORHEN based at Portsmouth and MOORFOWL at Devonport. Both vessels also undertake coastal work.

MV Warden

TRIALS VESSEL

Ship	Pennant Number	Completion Date	Builder
WARDEN	A368	1989	Richards

Displacement 626 tons **Dimensions** 48m x 10m x 4m **Speed** 15 knots **Complement** 11.

Notes
Built as a Range Maintenance Vessel but now based at Kyle of Lochalsh and operated by the RMAS in support of BUTEC. Note removal of gantry and extended bridge structure.

The RMAS have taken two further trials craft on long term charter to help with the various tasks at the Kyle of Lochalsh. These are the SARA MAATJE VI on charter from Van Stee of Holland and LENIE on charter from Maritime Craft Services of Scotland.

AIRCREW TRAINING VESSELS

Ship	Comp Date	Builder	Base Port
SMIT DEE	2003	BES Rosyth	Bukie
SMIT DART	2003	BES Rosyth	Plymouth
SMIT DON	2003	BES Rosyth	Blyth
SMIT YARE	2003	FBMA Cebu	Great Yarmouth
SMIT TOWY	2003	FBMA Cebu	Pembroke Dock
SMIT SPEY	2003	FBMA Cebu	Plymouth

G.R.T. 95.86 GRT **Dimensions** 27.6m x 6.6m x 1.5m **Speed** 21 knots **Complement** 6

Notes
The vessels were designed by FBM Babcock Marine and built in their shipyards in Scotland and the Philippines. Operated by SMIT International (Scotland) on behalf of the MoD for training military aircrew in marine survival techniques, helicopter winching drills and general marine support tasks. The design includes an aft docking well for a RIB or for torpedo recovery, a full width stern training platform and clear deck areas for helicopter winching drills. SMIT DART completed as a passenger vessel with larger superstructure. Two similar second-hand vessels, SMIT TAMAR and SMIT CYMYRAN are also employed in the same role. These vessels replaced the former RAF Spitfire class RTTLs in service.

• SMIT (SCOTLAND) LTD

• SMIT (SCOTLAND) LTD   **Smit Stour**

RANGE SAFETY VESSELS

Ship	Comp Date	Builder
SMIT STOUR	2003	Maritime Partners Norway
SMIT ROTHER	2003	Maritime Partners Norway
SMIT ROMNEY	2003	Maritime Partners Norway
SMIT CERNE	2003	Maritime Partners Norway
SMIT FROME	2003	Maritime Partners Norway
SMIT MERRION	2003	Maritime Partners Norway
SMIT PENALLY	2003	Maritime Partners Norway
SMIT WAY	2003	Maritime Partners Norway
SMIT NEYLAND	2003	Maritime Partners Norway

G.R.T. 7.0 GRT **Dimensions** 12.3m x 2.83m x 0.89m **Speed** 35 knots **Complement** 2

Notes
A new class of 12 metre Fast Patrol Craft which operate on Range Safety Duties at Dover, Portland and Pembroke. Have replaced the former RCT Sir and Honours class launches in this role.

RCTV Arezzo

RAMPED CRAFT LOGISTIC

Vessel	Pennant Number	Completion Date	Builder
ARROMANCHES	L105	1987	James & Stone
ANDALSNES	L107	1984	James & Stone
AKYAB	L109	1984	James & Stone
AACHEN	L110	1986	James & Stone
AREZZO	L111	1986	James & Stone
AUDEMER	L113	1987	James & Stone

Displacement 165 tons **Dimensions** 33m x 8m x 1.5m **Speed** 9 knots
Complement 6.

Notes
Smaller – "all purpose" landing craft capable of carrying up to 96 tons. In service in coastal waters around Cyprus and UK. ARROMANCHES was formerly AGHEILA (re-named 1994 when original vessel was sold). Several vessels sport green and black camouflage scheme.

AIRCRAFT OF THE FLEET AIR ARM

European Helicopter Industries EH101 MERLIN

Variants: HM1
Role: Anti-submarine and Maritime patrol
Engine: 3 x Rolls-Royce Turbomeca RTM322 turboshafts developing 2,100 shp
Length: 74' 10" Width: 14' 10" Height: 21' 10" Main rotor diameter: 61'
Max Speed: 167 kts   **Range:** 625 nm
Crew: 3 (Pilot, Observer and Aircrewman)
Avionics: Blue Kestrel 360 degree search radar, Orange Reaper ESM, passive and active sonar systems and AQS903 digital processor.
Armament: 4 lightweight torpedoes or depth charges.
Squadron service: 700M, 814, 820, 824 Squadrons
Notes: The Merlin HM1 is an advanced weapon system for the detection and attack of submarines that can also be operated in a number of other roles. Fast and agile for its size, Merlin can be flown by a single pilot and operate off both large and small ships' flight decks in high sea states and severe weather by day and night.
The first front line squadron, 814NAS, was operational in ARK ROYAL by late Spring 2002.

British Aerospace SEA HARRIER

Variants: FA2

Role: Short take off, vertical landing (STOVL) fighter attack and reconnaissance aircraft.

Engine: 1 x 21,500lb thrust Rolls Royce PEGASUS 104, turbofan.

Span 25' 3" **Length** 49' 1" **Height** 12' 0" **Max weight** 26,200lb.

Max speed Mach .9 540 knots **Crew** 1 pilot.

Avionics: Blue Vixen pulse doppler radar

Armament: Up to 4 x AMRAAM Air to Air Missiles. SIDEWINDER air to air missiles. 2 - 30mm Aden cannons with 120 rounds per gun in detachable pods, one either side of the lower fuselage. 1 fuselage centreline and 4 underwing hardpoints. The inner wing stations are capable of carrying 2,000lb of stores and are plumbed for drop tanks. The other positions can carry stores up to 1,000lb in weight. Possible loads include 1,000lb or practice bombs; 190 or 100 gallon drop tanks. A single F95 camera is mounted obliquely in the nose for reconnaissance.

Squadron Service: 800, 801 and 899 squadrons in commission.

Notes: On 1 April 2000, the Royal Navy's Sea Harriers joined the RAF's Harrier GR7s in Joint Force Harrier (JFH). The three Sea Harrier squadrons will continue to be based at Yeovilton but will start to run down in 2004 when 800 Squadron disbands, to be followed by 899 in 2005 and 801 in 2006. They will be replaced by Harrier GR9 aircraft in four squadrons, within JFH, two of which will be "dark blue" manned with the 800 and 801 squadron numbers.

• MoD/CROWN COPYRIGHT

Westland SEA KING

Developed for the Royal Navy from the Sikorsky SH3D, the basic Sea King airframe is used in three different roles. The following details are common to all:

Engines: 2 x 1600shp Rolls Royce Gnome H 1400 – 1 free power turbines.
Rotor Diameter 62' 0" **Length** 54' 9" **Height** 17' 2" **Max Weight** 21,400lb **Max Speed** 125 knots.

The 3 versions are:-

• DONALD DONALDSON

HAR 5 / HAS 6

The HAS6 has improved sonics, deeper dipping active sonar and ESM
Roles: Anti-submarine search and attack. SAR. Transport.
Crew: 2 pilots, 1 observer and 1 aircrewman.
Avionics: Sea Searcher radar; Type 2069 variable depth active/passive sonar AQS 902 passive sonobuoy analyser. Orange Crop passive ESM equipment.
Armament: 4 fuselage hardpoints capable of carrying STINGRAY torpedoes or depth charges. Various flares, markers, grenades and sonobuoys can be carried internally and hand launched. A 7.62mm machine gun can be mounted in the doorway.
Squadron Service: Five HAS6 aircraft are operated by 771 NAS, three for training and two Ships' Flights for Type 22 Frigates. 771 NAS also operates five HU5 aircraft, primarily in the Search and Rescue (SAR) role.
Notes: The Sea King has been the backbone of the Fleet Air Arm's anti-submarine force for more than 30 years but has now been superseded by the Merlin HM1. The HU5 continues to provide excellent SAR service in the south west approaches and at Prestwick, where three aircraft remain for SAR duties. Some HAS6 airframes, stripped of their radar and sonar, will be used by Commando squadrons while their HC4s are refurbished during 2004. Others, parented by 771 NAS at Culdrose, will be embarked in carriers for combat SAR and COD duties from 2004 onwards.

• MoD/CROWN COPYRIGHT

ASaC 7

Role: Airborne Early Warning. **Crew:** 1 pilot and 2 observers.
Avionics: Upgraded Thales Searchwater radar, Orange Crop passive ESM, Enhanced Communications System, Joint Tactical Information Distribution System (JTIDS)
Squadron Service: 849 HQ, 849A and 849B Flights in commission.
Notes: Used for the Airborne Surveillance and Control (ASaC) of the airspace over a maritime force. Can also be used for surface search utilising their sophisticated, computerised long range radar. During 2003 849A Flight was embarked in ARK ROYAL. 849HQ acts as a training and trials unit at Culdrose. There were 13 conversions of airframes to this role, two of which were lost during Operation Telic in the Gulf.

HC 4

Role: Commando assault and utility transport.
Crew: 2 pilots and 1 aircrewman.
Armament: Door mounted 7.62mm machine gun.
Squadron Service: 845, 846 and 848 Squadrons.
Notes: The HC4 has a fixed undercarriage with no sponsons or radome. It is equipped to carry up to 17 troops in the cabin or underslung loads up to 6000 lbs. The three Commando Support squadrons are based at Yeovilton but (together with 847 NAS with its Lynx and Gazelle aircraft) come under the command of the Joint Helicopter Command (JHC) based at Wilton, a tri-Service formation whose purpose is to maximise the effectiveness of all battlefield helicopters. The Commando Support squadrons train to operate in all environments, from arctic to tropical, and can embark or detach at short notice to support 3 Commando Brigade or as required by the JHC.

86

Westland LYNX

Variants: HAS 3, HMA 8, AH7.

Roles: Surface search and attack; anti-submarine attack; SAR; troop carrying.

Engines: 2 x 900hp Rolls Royce GEM BS 360-07-26 free shaft turbines.

Rotor diameter: 42' 0" **Length** 39' 1" **Height** 11' 0" **Max Weight** 9,500lb.

Max Speed: 150 knots. **Crew:** 1 pilot and 1 observer.

Avionics: SEA SPRAY radar. Orange Crop passive ESM equipment. Sea Owl Passive Infrared Device (Mk 8).

Armament: External pylons carry up to 4 - SEA SKUA air to surface missiles or 2 x STINGRAY torpedoes, depth charges and markers.

Squadron Service: 702 and 815 squadrons in commission.

Notes: Lynx OEU develops operational tactics for HMA 8 aircraft. 702 is the training squadron. 815 squadron is the parent unit for single aircraft ships flights. Both squadrons are based at Yeovilton. Ships' Flights are divided approximately equally between HAS 3 and HMA 8 aircraft. Another version of the Lynx, the AH7, is operated by 847 NAS in a Commando Support role. There are 35 airframes each of the HMA8 and HAS3 versions.

Royal Marine Gazelle AH1 (bottom) and Lynx AH7

Westland GAZELLE AH1

Engine: 1 x 592shp Turbomeca ASTAZOU free power turbine.
Crew: 1 or 2 pilots.

Notes: The Gazelle AH1 is used by 847 NAS based at Yeovilton as a spotter/communi-cations aircraft for the Royal Marines.

OTHER AIRCRAFT TYPES IN ROYAL NAVY SERVICE DURING 2004

• MoD/CROWN COPYRIGHT

British Aerospace HAWK

Engine: 1 x Adour Mk 151 5200 lbs thrust.
Crew: 1 or 2 Pilots (both service and civilian)
Notes: With Fleet Requirements and Aircraft Direction Unit (FRADU) at Culdrose to provide support for training of RN ships, RN Flying Standards Flight and as airborne targets for the Aircraft Direction School. The aircraft are operated by Babcock.

• MoD/CROWN COPYRIGHT

British Aerospace JETSTREAM T2 and T3

Engines: 2 x 940hp Turbomeca ASTAZOU 16D turboprops. (T3 Garrett turboprops).
Crew: 1 or 2 pilots, 2 student observers plus 3 other seats.
Notes: T2's are used by 750 Squadron at Culdrose for training Fleet Air Arm Observers. T3's are used by the 750 Heron flight at Yeovilton for operational support/communications flying.

• MoD/CROWN COPYRIGHT

Aerospatiale AS365N DAUPHIN 2

Engines: 2 x Turbomeca Arriel 1C1.
Crew: 1 or 2 pilots.
Notes: Operated by British International from Plymouth City Airport under MoD COMR (Civil Owned Military Registered) contract. Used to transfer Sea Training staff from shore and between ships operating in the Plymouth sea training areas during work-ups. Aircraft are also used for Guided Weapons System Calibration and Naval Gunfire Support.

GROB G115 D-2

Took over the flying grading and conversion of Rotary to Fixed Wing flying task from the Chipmunk. They are owned and operated by a division of Short Brothers plc and operate from Plymouth City Airport on behalf of 727 NAS (which formed on 6 December 2001).

Royal Navy Historic Flight

The RNHF is supported financially by the Swordfish Heritage Trust. The Historic Flight has been civilianised since 1993.

The current holding of aircraft is:

Flying: 1 Fairey Swordfish.
Under Repair: 2 Fairey Swordfish, 1 Sea Hawk, 1 Sea Fury.

WEAPONS OF THE ROYAL NAVY

Sea Launched Missiles

◀ Trident II D5

The American built Lockheed Martin Trident 2 (D5) submarine launched strategic missiles are Britain's only nuclear weapons and form the UK contribution to the NATO strategic deterrent. 16 missiles, each capable of carrying up to 6 UK manufactured thermonuclear warheads (but currently limited to 4 under current government policy), are aboard each of the Vanguard class SSBNs. Trident has a maximum range of 12,000 km and is powered by a three stage rocket motor. Launch weight is 60 tonnes, overall length and width are 13.4 metres and 2.1 metres respectively.

Sea Wolf

Short range rapid reaction anti-missile and anti-aircraft weapon. The complete weapon system, including radars and fire control computers, is entirely automatic in operation. Type 22 frigates carry two sextuple Sea Wolf launchers but the subsequent Type 23 frigates carry 32 Vertical Launch Seawolf (VLS) in a silo on the foredeck. Basic missile data: weight 82 kg, length 1.9 m, wingspan 56 cm, range c.56 km, warhead 13.4 kg. The VLS missile is basically similar but has jettisonable tandem boost rocket motors.

Harpoon

The Boeing (McDonnell Douglas) Harpoon is a sophisticated anti-ship missile using a combination of inertial guidance and active radar homing to attack targets out to a range of 130 km, cruising at Mach 0.9 and carrying a 227 kg warhead. Currently fitted to the Batch II Type 22 and Type 23 frigates. It is powered by a lightweight turbojet but is accelerated at launch by a booster rocket. The Royal Navy also deploys the UGM-84 submarine launched version aboard its Swiftsure and Trafalgar class SSNs.

Sea Dart

A medium range area defence anti aircraft missile powered by a ramjet and solid fuel booster rocket. Maximum effective range is in the order of 80 km and the missile accelerates to a speed of Mach 3.5. It forms the main armament of the Type 42 destroyers. Missile weight 550 kg, length 4.4 m, wingspan 0.91 m.

Tomahawk (BGM-109)

This is a land attack cruise missile with a range of 1600 km and can be launched from a variety of platforms including surface ships and submarines. Some 65 of the latter version were purchased from America to arm Trafalgar class SSNs with the first being delivered to the Royal Navy for trials during 1998. Tomahawk is fired in a disposal container from the submarine's conventional torpedo tubes and is then accelerated to its subsonic cruising speed by a booster rocket motor before a lightweight F-107 turbojet takes over for the cruise. Its extremely accurate guidance system means that small targets can be hit with precision at maximum range, as was dramatically illustrated in the Gulf War and Afghanistan. Total weight of the submarine version, including its launch capsule is 1816 kg, it carries a 450 kg warhead, length is 6.4 metres and wingspan (fully extended) 2.54 m. Fitted in some S and T class submarines.

Air Launched Missiles

Sea Skua

A small anti ship missile developed by British Aerospace arming the Lynx helicopters carried by various frigates and destroyers. The missile weighs 147 kg, has a length of 2.85 m and a span of 62 cm. Powered by solid fuel booster and sustainer rocket motors, it has a range of over 15 km at high subsonic speed. Sea Skua is particularly effective against patrol vessels and fast attack craft, as was demonstrated in both the Falklands and Gulf Wars.

Sidewinder

This is one of the world's most successful short range air to air missiles. The latest AIM-9L version carried by Sea Harriers uses a heat seeking infra red guidance system and has a range of 18 km. Powered by a solid fuel rocket motor boosting it to speeds of Mach 2.5, it weighs 86.6 kg and is 2.87 m long.

AMRAAM

The Hughes AIM-120 Advanced Medium Range Air To Air Missile arms the latest Sea Harrier FA.2 and has a range of around 50 km. Weight 157 kg, length 3.65 m. Coupled with the Blue Vixen multi mode radar, the AMRAAM gives a substantial boost to the aircraft's capability as an air defence interceptor, allowing Beyond Visual Range (BVR) engagements.

Guns

114mm Vickers Mk8

The Royal Navy's standard medium calibre general purpose gun which arms the later Type 22s, Type 23 frigates and Type 42 destroyers. Rate of fire: 25 rounds/min. Range: 22,000 m. Weight of Shell: 21 kg.

Goalkeeper

A highly effective automatic Close in Weapons System (CIWS) designed to shoot down missiles and aircraft which have evaded the outer layers of a ships defences. The complete system, designed and built in Holland, is on an autonomous mounting and includes radars, fire control computers and a 7-barrel 30 mm Gatling gun firing 4200 rounds/min. Goalkeeper is designed to engage targets between 350 and 1500 metres away.

Phalanx

A US built CIWS designed around the Vulcan 20 mm rotary cannon. Rate of fire is 3000 rounds/min and effective range is c.1500 m. Fitted in Type 42, HM Ships OCEAN and FEARLESS.

GCM-AO3 30mm

This mounting carries two Oerlikon 30 mm guns each capable of firing 650 rounds/min. Effective range is 3000 m. Fitted to Type 22 frigates and the LPDs.

DS30B 30mm

Single 30 mm mounting carrying an Oerlikon 30 mm gun. Fitted to Type 23 frigates and various patrol vessels and MCMVs.

GAM BO 20mm

A simple hand operated mounting carrying a single Oerlikon KAA 200 automatic cannon firing 1000 rounds/min. maximum range is 2000 m. Carried by most of the fleet's major warships except the Type 23 frigates.

20mm Mk.7A

The design of this simple but reliable weapon dates back to World War II but it still provides a useful increase in firepower, particularly for auxiliary vessels and RFAs. Rate of fire 500-800 rounds/min.

Torpedoes

Stingray

A lightweight anti submarine torpedo which can be launched from ships, helicopters or aircraft. In effect it is an undersea guided missile with a range of 11 km at 45 knots or 7.5 km at 60 knots. Length 2.1 m, diameter 330 mm. Aboard Type 42s and Type 22s Stingray is fired from triple tubes forming part of the Ships Torpedo Weapon System (STWS) but the newer Type 23s have the Magazine Torpedo Launch System (MTLS) with internal launch tubes.

Mk24 Tigerfish

A wire guided heavyweight torpedo carried by all Royal Navy submarines. Mainly designed for the anti-submarine role but its 134 kg warhead is equally effective against surface vessels. Propulsion is by means of a powerful two speed electric motor giving a range of 29 km at 24 knots or 13 km at 35 knots. Diameter is the standard 533 mm, and overall length approximately 6.5 m.

Spearfish

A complex heavyweight torpedo now entering service after a protracted and extensive development period. Claimed by the manufacturers to be the world's fastest torpedo, capable of over 70 kts, its sophisticated guidance system includes an onboard acoustic processing suite and tactical computer backed up by a command and control wire link to the parent submarine. Spearfish is fired from the standard submarine torpedo tube, but it is slightly shorter than Tigerfish and utilises an advanced turbine engine for higher performance.

At the end of the line ...

Readers may well find other warships afloat which are not mentioned in this book. The majority have fulfilled a long and useful life and are now relegated to non-seagoing duties. The following list gives details of their current duties:

Pennant No	Ship	Remarks
	BRITANNIA	Ex Royal Yacht at Leith. Open to the public.
	CAROLINE	RNR Drill Ship at Belfast, Northern Ireland.
A134	RAME HEAD	Escort Maintenance Vessel – Royal Marines Training Ship in Fareham Creek (Portsmouth)
C35	BELFAST	World War II Cruiser Museum ship – Pool of London. Open to the public daily . Tel: 020 7940 6300
D23	BRISTOL	Type 82 Destroyer – Sea Cadet Training Ship at Portsmouth.
D73 S17	CAVALIER OCELOT	World War II Destroyer & Oberon class Submarine Museum Ships at Chatham. Partially open to the public. Tel: 01634 823800
F126 S21 M1115	PLYMOUTH ONYX BRONINGTON	Type 12 Frigate, Oberon class Submarine & Ton class Minesweeper. Museum Ships at Birkenhead, Wirral. Open to the public daily. Tel: 0151 650 1573
S67	ALLIANCE	Submarine – Museum Ship at Gosport Open to the public daily. Tel: 023 92 511349
M1151 M1154	IVESTON KELLINGTON	(Thurrock) } Static Sea Cadet (Stockton upon Tees) } Training Vessels

At the time of publishing (December 2003) the following ships were laid up in long term storage or awaiting sale.

PORTSMOUTH: Intrepid; Fearless; Boxer; Brave; Coventry; London; Bridport.

PLYMOUTH: Splendid, Courageous; Conqueror; Valiant; Warspite.

ROSYTH: Resolution; Renown; Repulse; Revenge; Swiftsure; Dreadnought; Churchill.